HIPSTER ANIMALS

HIPSTER ANIMALS

»—————→ ## A FIELD GUIDE ←—————«

DYNA MOE

Ten Speed Press
Berkeley

CONTENTS

AUTHOR'S NOTE

Depending on when in the cycle of coolness you bought/
stole/downloaded this book, you might find it to be a
razor-sharp codification of people you know, hopelessly
out of touch, a charming time capsule of your youth, or
on the verge of experiencing a comeback. Welcome.

The species included within are not meant to represent
the full spectrum of youth cultures (no dudebros, no
mainline geekery, no music-genre-specific cults) but
rather a narrow sliver of beasts of the postcollege
upwardly mobile special-snowflakes animal kingdom
and those who want to be them.

The author does not wish to convey judgment or imply
that one species (mentioned or unmentioned) is better
than another but rather to say that we all are equally
repulsive. Everyone is the worst.

FOOD & DRINK

FARM-TO-TABLE WAITER

They're not really a waiter, y'know. Not sure what else they are but they're less about bringing you what you ask for than being a facilitator between your wants and what's best for the whole biosphere.

MARKINGS
An earthy, ultra-sincere manner that reflects the possibilities of fresh, local, locally fresh food.

CALL
" . . . with organic ultra-local *fines herbes* harvested from the windowsill of the bathroom upstairs."

HABITAT
Dining rooms paneled in reclaimed barn wood and lit with Edison bulbs; definitely not the "farm" part of the equation.

DIET
At work: staff meal at 4 p.m.; at home: industrial tubs of condiments and mustard greens stolen from walk-in fridge.

SPOOR
Basic comfort food meals, familiar to everyone, with every ingredient replaced with an artisanal, sustainable equivalent (market price).

HOST SPECIES
Ex-CEO who quit the rat race to micro-focus on heritage livestock or semi-endangered cheese somewhere "upstate."

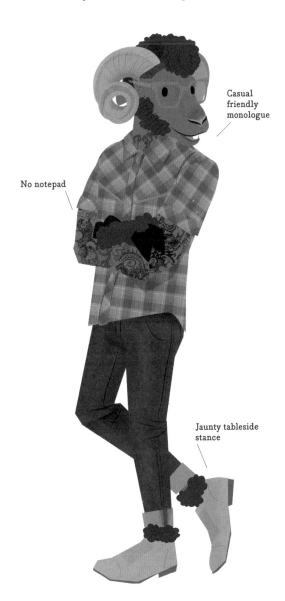

Casual friendly monologue

No notepad

Jaunty tableside stance

KRAFT BRÜE KNOW-IT-ALL

Beer is the great leveler. Everyone likes beer. Beer welcomes all comers. But what if beer could be as top-loaded with terminology, snobbery, and trivia to be used a litmus test of self-worth as fine wines are? Done.

Oh, you like cask ale, huh? I hear that's getting popular with *some* people

Secretly has the alcohol tolerance of a third grader

MARKINGS
A jaunty European attitude toward drunken one-upmanship.

CALL
"I can really taste the hops."

HABITAT
Nouveau biergartens: like a backyard BBQ writ large with more aggressively sloshed strangers.

DIET
Aside from beer? Mostly mustard.

NEST
Kitted out in Euro football memorabilia—scarves, jerseys, World Cup sticker albums, coasters—and an odd smell.

FUN FACT
Descended from home microbrewers, jettisoning vestigial ponytail and attempts to bottle their very own brand from a still in the closet.

WARNING
Accidentally poisoned friends with home-brewed kvass, never apologized.

DANDY MIXOLOGIST

Sidle up to a reclaimed zinc bar, take a seat on a reproduction Bauhaus stool, order a Sazerac, and get an earful about what you really should have ordered.

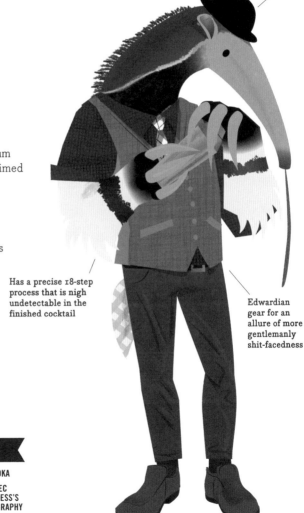

Hat

MARKINGS
Waistcoats. This species is the primary consumer of waistcoats.

CALL
"Top shelf . . . small batch . . . copper kettle . . . all our bitters were brewed on site."

HABITAT
Lounges without signs, simulacrum dive bars with an excess of reclaimed barn wood and Edison bulbs.

DIET
Kirsch-soaked morello cherries, citron wedges, charcuterie scraps off a chunk of slate.

THREATS
Secondhand cirrhosis.

SPOOR
Letterpressed menu where every drink is named after a line of symbolist poetry.

Has a precise 18-step process that is nigh undetectable in the finished cocktail

Edwardian gear for an allure of more gentlemanly shit-facedness

TOP INFUSED VODKA FLAVORS

VICTORY	CORMORANT	VODKA
GUANCIALE	CHICORY	ALEC GUINNESS'S FILMOGRAPHY
BABKA	SLEEPYTIME®	
BRUNCH		

CITY BOY BBQ PITMASTER

Shunning the traditional regional definitions of barbecue (KC, Memphis, the Carolinas, Texas) for highly specialized micro-regions like "north Kentucky panhandle" and "11th Eleventh and Branch Street," further supplemented with winsome application of East Asian flavors. Kimchi? Fish sauce? Yes, we daikon!

The secret is RC Cola. Even in the salad

With the right attitude, anything can be made into a pickle

MARKINGS
Co-opted jungle camo of a redneck rube, but has written a dissertation on the social ramifications contained therein.

CALL
"It's served in a Mason jar."

HABITAT
Rustic but minimal; bleached pine wainscoting.

DIET
Inexplicably, just became a vegan.

LIFE CYCLE
Spends the first two decades trying to get out of some hillbilly shithole town; now re-creating it for foodie patrons in cities with good public transportation networks and bike lanes.

MIGRATION PATTERN

ONE-OFF FESTIVAL BOOTH

(REPEAT CYCLE)

FOOD TRUCK

CROWED-SOURCED FUNDRAISING APPEAL

POP-UP

CLOSED BY HEALTH DEPARTMENT (INEVITABLE)

FOOD HALL STALL

FULL RESTAURANT

PHO AUTHENTICITY POLICE

Deriving authority from a stopover in Hanoi during a college package trip, they can tell you exactly where it went wrong.

MARKINGS
Visible eye-rolling disgust at "corruptions" to "mainstream palates."

CALL
Can slurp and exasperatedly tut at the same time.

HABITAT
Strip mall restaurants with the hygiene standard of bus-station toilets.

DIET
Puts Sriracha (made in Irwindale, California) on cornflakes yet throws a shit-fit if there's not-indigenous-to-originating-region plant matter in soup.

TEMPERAMENT
To dining companions: patronizing; to food: weary disappointment.

RANGE
The Pho type is one of a wide-ranging family of Authenticity Police subspecies. Behaviors and markings are similar but range varies.

FUN FACT
Even gluten-free paleo-vegans are embarrassed by how they bully waiters with ingredient questions.

Not Vietnamese

Avoids any name with a pho pun in it

Don't you dare offer a fork

KNOW YOUR FOOD TRUCKS

Food trucks rose from state-fair misery to gentrified urban hallmarks years ago. The appeal isn't hard to see: they combine the convenience of a mobile kitchen with the means to skip town when massive food poisoning breaks out!

However, their widespread success has led to a glut of uninteresting diversification. To differentiate a cutting-edge mobile food operation from some mass-appeal clunker for businessmen's lunch breaks, the food truck's name *must* be an inappropriate pun (clunky or reference-y) or a winking allusion to something unpleasant, and the menu must be micro-focused on one item.

EXPERIMENTAL COFFEE GASTRONOMIST

Specialty coffee has flourished in the last decade, but in the opinion of this species, it has been bogged down by immature candy-coated gimmickry rather than pushing the frontiers of beverage-as-art.

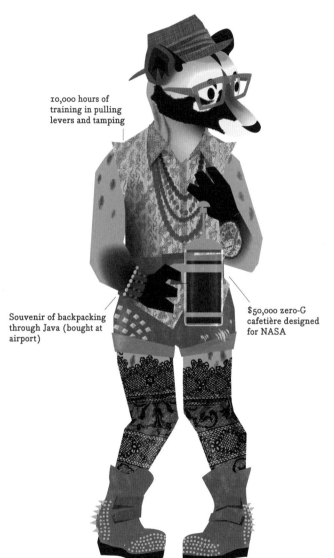

10,000 hours of training in pulling levers and tamping

Souvenir of backpacking through Java (bought at airport)

$50,000 zero-G cafetière designed for NASA

MARKINGS
Tamping blisters; steam-jet dueling scars.

CALL
"Would you like truffled fleur de sel dusted topping for $1 extra?"

HABITAT
Behind the counter of shop named after a part of the plant, steps of production, or accoutrements of coffee (The Steeping Bean, The Grind, Mill & Stamen) rendered on window glass in gilded Victorian lettering.

DIET
Foam, fumes, and jittery nerves.

BEHAVIOR
Despite near-constant caffeine rush by proximity, this species is rarely aggressive but inclined toward apologetic, mumbling introversion when addressing non-coffee-machine entities.

THREATS
National brand chain hegemony.

FUN FACT
This species can tell a French press Americano from a cold brew espresso based only on *the sound*.

TOMORROW'S COFFEE TRENDS

LEMONAFFEE	COLUMBIAN ARNOLD PALMER
KOFFUCHA	COFFEE + KOMBUCHA
CARDAMOMIATO	CARDAMOM + WATER (NO COFFEE)
SALTED COFFEE	SELF-EXPLANATORY
VOLCANANO AKA EYJAFJALLAJÖKULLATTE	ICELANDIC HOT SPRING—GROWN BEANS ROASTED IN GEOTHERMAL OVENS
FLATTEST WHITE	MICROFOAM SO SMALL THAT IT LACKS A 3RD DIMENSION, SERVED IN THE TRADITIONAL ANTIPODEAN STYLE (CUP UPSIDE DOWN)
BILLWACCINO	DISTILLLED FROM COFFEE PASSED THROUGH THE SWEAT GLANDS OF AA MEMBERS FOR A MELLOWER, MORE REMORSEFUL PROFILE
AN EMPTY CUP	

F YOU! TIP ME! NO FARTHINGS

HALF & HALF OAT MILK URINE

MOTORLOAN LIVE! FESTIFEST! PARADE

VEGAN GELATO SCOOPER

A provider of treats that evoke the innocence of childhood yoked to a very adult awareness that—unless one consciously opts out—the world is built on exploitation and cruelty with sprinkles on top.

Humanely sourced conflict-free ugly-ass old lady glasses

Arrowroot, agar-agar, and moral soundness

Made from cotton plants that died peacefully of old age in bed

Spectacular ass

Eco slip-ons not unlike those issued to inmates who can't be trusted with shoelaces

MARKINGS
A gentle manner that would never exploit any species for their own gain; rickets.

CALL
Doesn't call their sweetheart "honey"; it endorses exploitation of bees. (Prefers the pet name "agave nectar.")

HABITAT
Cruelty-free but quaintness-filled. No living creature inconvenienced for the antique-filled ambience.

DIET
Coconut milk, frozen bananas, avocado pulp, soy dust, and pistachio paste.

MIGRATION
Gelato is feeling a little played out; switching over to Taiwanese snow ice next summer.

FUN FACT
That beetroot flavor? The bright red one? It's actually made of blood. Sorry.

NEW WAVE PIZZAIOLO

Acts on the noble goal of bringing decent pizza to pizza deserts like St. Louis (processed provolone on matzo is not a pizza, St. Louis); charges ignoble prices for the result.

MARKINGS
Piercing eyes that have looked into the abyss and stuck a pizza in it.

CALL
"Of course the middle is still gooey. That's authentic. In Naples, pizza is considered a soup."

HABITAT
Within eyebrow-singeing distance of a 5,000° oven.

DIET
Cynar and Limonata shots; Dunhills; *fior di latte* that fell on the floor.

HOST SPECIES
Pho Authenticity Police, page 7.

WARNING
Docile until you ask for toppings substitutions on chef-designed pizza offerings. Those combinations are infallible; may provoke an attack.

If the crust is not charred black, how will you know it came from a brick oven?

Wood-fired wrist burns

This isn't some grab-and-go slice; we employ *graphic design*

COMMUNITY VEGETABLE ADVOCATE

If they aren't too busy with guerrilla gardening on highway medians or stretching the definition of what can be categorized as "a salad," this species will gladly inform you of how superior local produce is to supermarket greens. Usually, you don't even have to ask.

HOLY SHIT! RAMPS!

Stew it maybe? Does it pickle well?

This is just for looking at, not eating.

Is this cabbage? Smells like cabbage. I'm calling it cabbage.

MARKINGS
Hempen, home-knit, or Dumpster-dived clothes; "Vegans Do It Harmlessly" patch; berry stains.

CALL
Way more vocally enthusiastic about root vegetables than anyone really should be.

HABITAT
CSA farm share drop-offs; green markets at the crack of dawn before the farmers get there.

DIET
Nothing more than 10 miles from source unless it's avocados. Oh, how they love an avocado!

THREATS
Restaurateurs that buy up all the strawberries before the market officially opens.

MATING
Has felt a sexual stirring at the sight of a particularly symmetrical butternut squash.

SPOOR
Droplets of organic waste matter from leaky hemp bag on the way to the community compost bin.

TRIVIA SMÖRGÅSBORD

SIGNATURE GELATO FLAVORS

- ★ STARFRUIT STRACCIATELLA
- ★ SZECHUAN PEPPERCORN
- ★ SALTED GIANDUJA
- ★ BARIUM ENEMA
- ★ MASTIC

- ★ CILANTRO/SOAP
- ★ ANEMIA
- ★ WET EARTH
- ★ MIASMA
- ★ SADNESS

ARTISANAL PIZZA TOPPING COMBINATIONS

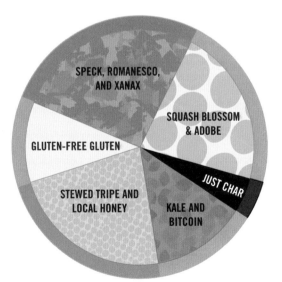

SPECK, ROMANESCO, AND XANAX

SQUASH BLOSSOM & ADOBE

GLUTEN-FREE GLUTEN

JUST CHAR

STEWED TRIPE AND LOCAL HONEY

KALE AND BITCOIN

WHAT TO GET AT THE FARMER'S MARKET

SMUG SUPERIORITY

LUKEWARM, EXPENSIVE, "HUMANE" MEAT FROM A COOLER FULL OF MELTED ICE

I DON'T KNOW WHAT THIS IS BUT IT'S LOCAL

TOMATOES WITH ECZEMA

GOURDS THAT LOOK LIKE "AFTER" PICTURES IN STD SCARE FILMS

HONEY THAT COSTS MORE THAN BLOOD PLASMA

KALE

MORE KALE

ON THE SCENE

UGH THIS GUY AGAIN

We all know one.

MARKINGS
Is he serious with those glasses? Ick.

CALL
Wait. *This* guy?

HABITAT
Oh god, really? *Really?*

DIET
Not him again.

PREDATORS
Huh? Why? Wha—?

NEST
This guy?

THREATS
I can't believe anyone would
intentionally . . .

SPOOR
I can't even . . . man . . .

RANGE
No, wait, you're joking, right?

He has to
know, right?

Is this on
purpose?

Yeah, I think
he's in on it

RECREATIONALLY HOMELESS

Homelessness brought on by mental illness, drug abuse, poverty, and disenfranchisement is a tragedy, but maaaan, do the homeless have a lot of street cred, and this species wants in on the action.

Full sleeves of new tattoos paid for with Mom's credit card

Cupertino's latest model

Contains: J.Crew school uniform

MARKINGS
A veneer of gutter-borne filth over solidly middle-class suburban core.

CALL
"Hey! Fuck you! Gimme a cigarette."

HABITAT
Main thoroughfare near university neighborhood; Food Not Bombs potlucks; Occupy encampments; sidewalk in front of dollar pizza/kebab joints.

(Not found in: church soup kitchens; rehab centers; public libraries.)

DIET
Dumpster-dived restaurant scraps; fruit stolen from community garden; campus cafeteria buffet (snuck in).

NEST
Filled with items scavenged from dorm clean-out day.

PREDATORS
Former prep school classmates "outing" them; the involuntarily homeless.

WARNING
Do not approach! Prone to lash out indiscriminately; has nothing else to do.

BRAZEN KIDULT

The blueprint for this species' adult lifestyle was drafted after a blowout argument with Mom at age nine, the thesis of which was that if they were a grown up, they could do whatever they wanted and stay up as late as they wanted and watch as much TV as they wanted and there wouldn't be anything Mom could do about it . . . plus drugs.

MARKINGS
All the identifiers of an overindulged toddler blown up to grown-up size.

CALL
Enthusiastic use of words like *nummy* despite being legally allowed to vote and drive.

HABITAT
Glow-in-the-dark star stickers on the ceiling, plastic dinos on the shelves, and original Sears *Star Wars* duvet in an ultra-luxe loft-style condo complex.

DIET
A cross-section of his stomach would be identical to that of a birthday party piñata seized by border customs: mostly candy . . . plus drugs.

FUN FACT
Makes $100K+ a year, somehow.

THREATS
"As young as you feel" can't disguise age-based macular denegration.

Halloween costume, clothes . . . same diff

Tastes never change

SELF-ELECTED ARBITER OF TASTE

This species has heard of everything you've probably never heard of and will tell you so with no embarrassment.

The designer made it for me . . . we're tight

You wouldn't know this brand

Yeah, had this custom-made— only one like it

MARKINGS
Effortless cool.

CALL
(Derisive snort.)

HABITAT
This great neighborhood, totally ungentrified, that's not even on anyone's radar yet but in a year will be the absolute ground zero for the scene.

DIET
Stuff you can't, like, just pick up at any supermarket. He has a "guy" and gets it delivered.

SPOOR
"I'm over this now. You can have it."

THREATS
Obsolescence.

TWENTY-FIRST-CENTURY GENTRY

Despite humble roots, dresses like a captain of industry from a Technicolor western. Bringing back "aristocrat louche" while the real 1%-ers don fleeces and cargo shorts.

MARKINGS
Turned out like a P. G. Wodehouse acid trip; "Dressed up like a million dollar trooper, tryin' hard to look like Gary Cooper (super duper)."

CALL
"Heritage brand" . . . "True Prep" . . . "Take Ivy". . .

HABITAT
Speakeasy-style hidden-entry whiskey bars; nouveau haberdasheries; Japanese street-style photography blogs.

SPOOR
Ambergris-based pomade packaged in a recycled cigar tin; ivory-handled walking-stick-cum-USB-drive.

THREATS
Tagged Facebook photos of high school "emo phase"; seersucker vest deliberately "lost" by "willfully obtuse" dry cleaner.

PREDATORS
See Dandy Mixologist, page 5, entangling them with the allure of old-fashioned drinks with new-fashioned prices—$17 shandies, fizz-whimsies, Darbyshires Idylls.

Celphie-lopod

Oh, this isn't a trend; I need it for my slight astigmatism

Can open a jar of Gentleman's Relish

Pattern mixing is for amateurs; this is full-on pattern particle accelerating

PROXIMITY IRRITANT

In the high-density desirable neighborhoods almost all species prefer, the lack of living space can grind a nerve. This species specializes in doing it.

Stupid mouth

Stupid gesture

Stupid hat

Stupid shirt

Stupid leggings

MARKINGS
Mindlessly appropriated ethnic accessories; stupid tattoos; tight-ass pants.

CALL
Loud/relentless. Question intonation on nonquestion statements and vocal fry.

HABITAT
Blocking your view at the show, sitting at the next table at the bar . . . somehow always within earshot.

DIET
Eaten with mouth open, while yell-talking into hands-free cell.

SPOOR
Litters like it was nothing. Just leaving shit all over the place.

MATING
Screamy, banging lovemaking that can be heard through paper-thin apartment walls.

NEST
Apartment above yours. Stomps around in heels (tap shoes?!) at all hours.

FUN FACT
Inexplicably singled out as a representative of your generation in media coverage.

FEMAN-ISH FLAMEWARRIOR

The modern descendants of suffragettes who hurled themselves under racehorses use the full power of Internet anonymity to attempt to bring about gender equality by being assholes.

MARKINGS

Designed to please xirself. Not for your pleasure, Hitler!

CALL

Trigger warnings; entitlement accusations; rage-splaining.

HABITAT

A postgender, ambisexual, pronoun-inclusive paradigm. Not like yours, Hitler!

DIET

Social justice. Look into it, Hitler!

PREY

Hetero-neurotypical non-poly binary cis "males"; ignorant teenagers on social media (other than themselves, of course).

PREDATORS

Professional bloggers who actually advocate for disenfranchised populations rather than their idealized notion of disenfranchised populations; zerself in five years.

LIFE CYCLE

As wider society warms up to hir cause, ze switches to another repressed demographic (or makes one up) to be offended on behalf of.

Fixing society by constantly accusing everyone else of being a part of the problem

This machine kills fascists

SHAMING

CHECK YOUR PRIVILEGE

A tribute to exploited populations; totally *not* appropriation, okay?

ROGUE BIKETAVIST

Also known to drivers as the "critical masshole."

Franken-bike of cannibalized parts held together with grip tape

Factors weekly bike theft into living expenses

Uneven cuffs identifies a fledged adult

MARKINGS
Sweat-soaked thrifted polyester; a chain that could raise the *Bismarck*; largely symbolic helmet hanging off belt.

CALL
Bitching about sponsored bike-share program amateurs and weekend pleasure cyclists despite professed goal of expanding bike use in the city.

HABITAT
Anywhere but the designated bike lane. Flouting The Man's hangups about "going the right way" in traffic.

MIGRATION
On major roads in massive flocks where they change society by reducing traffic flow to a snail's pace.

THREATS
Double-parked cars; plate glass; car doors.

FUN FACT
So determined to prove cars are unnecessary, once delivered a piano to a sixth-floor walkup by cycle.

TRUSTAFARIAN DICKWAD

All the other scions of its tax bracket are bores, so they want to slum with the common kids and sow some oats. They would absolutely rather die than work at the family firm (at least until they're too old to party).

MARKINGS
Top-quality stuff that they don't take care of.

CALL
Something offensive that belies the privileged roots they're oblivious to.

HABITAT
Lives in filth, grew up with a housekeeper, and really doesn't know how to clean anything.

DIET
Always eats out but never tips. Doesn't believe in it.

THREATS
When the 99% finally rise up, this guy will be first up against the wall. Despite their slumming familiarity. Probably because of their slumming familiarity.

BEHAVIOR
Uses time to work on their "art," which may or may not exist, but living life is an art form.

MATING
Always flaunts their downwardly mobile working class significant other right in their parents' hypocritical faces (oblivious to how their date feels about it).

Slumming! In a $5,000/month studio!

"My friends back home would just *die* if they knew I was drinking domestic."

Has boarding school crest tattooed on his goolies

Thrifted! Just like a real poor person would do!

GLOBE-TROTTING SEEKER-OF-SELF

Y'know that movie Eat Pray Love? *Like that but with a young cool Zooey Deschanel instead of lame old Julia Roberts. And more diarrhea.*

Developed a taste for grass seed jelly on last trip to the East

Haggled for at the open-air market despite not speaking the language (may be cursed with their quaint folk religion. So authentic!)

Sensible European-style walking sandals

MARKINGS
Trucker tan lines; poorly hidden traveler's checks from parents; gauzy linen pants.

CALL
English. Enthusiastic and with gestures. They'll get understood eventually.

HABITAT
"The open road."

DIET
What the locals eat. Super open-minded and nonjudgmental. (Has gotten dysentery nine times.)

MATING
An exotic stranger for just one night but will never ever tire of telling the story for years to come.

RANGE
Bumming around Eastern European hostels; an endangered/abused species refuge near Angkor Wat; Africa (nonspecific . . . just "Africa").

SPOOR
A trail of digital photos smiling in front of the cultural achievements of civilizations that actually did something with their time.

PORTMANTEAU-N APPÉTIT:
the joy of food mash-ups

Combining two geographically isolated cuisines into one portable food item has been a runaway success for the Korean taco, the Ramen Burger, and the Cronut™, but the potential match-ups are infinite. Any food truckers worth their Himalayan pink salt can stick a skewer at random into a globe and come up with the next big thing.

KIM-CHEESE
Your choice of cheese + Korean pickled cabbage grilled toasties

CROISANTERÍA
Breakfast pastry infused with syncretized Caribbean folk religion

WOBEGACHOS
Minnesota-Mexican lutefisk, hotdish + queso over tortilla chips

Ceci n'est pas une མོག་མོག་

POMO MOMO
Poststructuralist, deconstructed Tibetan dumplings

"This tastiness is abjectly real."
—S. Žižek

BBQ PULLED BJORK WITH A SIDE OF HÁKARL SLAW
Reykjavík meets Memphis; the Sugarcubes meet sweet tea

ESCARGOGURT
Fine French cuisine pulverized into a fine paste, served in *un cylindre squeezable*

MAKE YOUR OWN: _____ + _____ = _____

FASHION & STYLE

FASHION PLATE PHOTO DIARIST

*If a phenomenon is not observed, then it can't be proved to exist,
and these shoes are too phenomenal to be theoretical.*

MARKINGS
Totes on trend.

CALL
Expertly worded compliment-fishing
disguised as self-deprecation ("Don't
look at my hair, it's a mess"; "I hate
myself . . . I'm a cancer on the
world.").

HABITAT
Second bedroom used as walk-in
closet . . . to dismay of roommate
living in it.

DIET
Ugh. I'm sooooo fat. Don't look
at these 3,000 photos of me.

SPOOR
GPYs, 1 OOTDs, 2 and TBTs3 when
feeling nostalgic, but they're all just
DCFA.

BEHAVIOR
Spends majority of time preparing
and documenting outfits and never
actually wears them anywhere.

HOST SPECIES
Accepts payola in crop top form from
soft-marketing arm of online vendors.

WARNING
No social media update in
24 hours = presume dead.

Classic slimming
bent-arm pose,
jutting of chin

Photo posts
accompanied by
quotation from
Unaffiliated Religion
Ambiguously
Inspirational Daily
Calendar

Clues in background of
photo (framed degree,
baby) suggest individual
is far older than assumed

SNEAKER FREAK

Never does anything remotely athletic—a molecule of perspiration or a sudden breeze might downgrade the gear from "Near Mint" to "Good."

Inwardly ecstatic over being mistaken for a dance crew member on the street

Favorite color: "limited edition"

Spends more time adjusting Velcro to be just right than they would tying laces

MARKINGS
Supa-dope.

CALL
Clunky made-in-Asia "Engrish" brand names that they see absolutely nothing funny about.

HABITAT
In line. On line. A line.

DIET
Doesn't eat; saving all money for next fashion house + cartoon character collab.

THREATS
Job application to sole domestic outlet for Japanese import streetwear "pending further review" when this species asked where new arrivals are kept and under how much security.

NEST
Padded with mint-in-boxes stacked like cordwood.

PREDATOR
Brands who keep reissuing the same kicks with slight variations year after year, taking advantage of completist compulsion.

NAIL ART TUTORIAL QUEEN

Using the interconnectivity of the digital (double meaning, there) world allows this species to not only show off their fingertip assets but also gain acolytes willing to mimic and pay homage to their craft.

MARKINGS
Spectacular talons—the size and complexity of display express fitness and dominance; a perky on-camera demeanor describing the process of making them.

CALL
"Macro glitter flake . . .";
"three-way prismatic iridescence . . .";
"magnetized texture crème . . .";
"crackle top coat . . ."

HABITAT
An appointment-only salon run out of her studio apartment, in front of her webcam.

DIET
Finger foods.

SPOOR
Whiff of acetone; spilled glitter trail.

THREATS
Inability to use touchscreens.

NEST
Fortress of varnish, polish, and gel in choice of lustre: vitreous, adamantine, pearly, silky, resinous, metallic or matte.

This one's a sticker!

Own brand of small-batch handmade custom-mixed lacquer

The rage style in Shinsaibashi; copied out of the newest issue of *Let's Nail: Super*スワロ*!*

Just enough self-justification that she's "using her art history degree"

FILTH FASHION MODEL

Aspiring to Warhol's Factory but landing in the bedraggled chorus of an amateur production of Rent, *this is what happened to those quiet kids in the back of art class.*

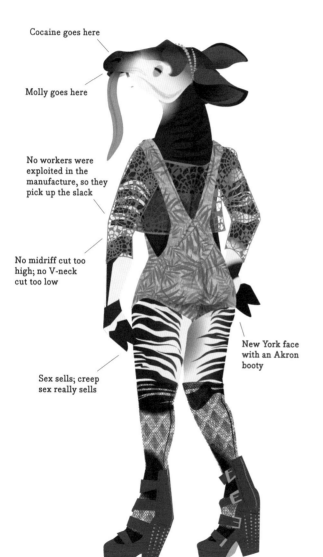

Cocaine goes here

Molly goes here

No workers were exploited in the manufacture, so they pick up the slack

No midriff cut too high; no V-neck cut too low

Sex sells; creep sex really sells

New York face with an Akron booty

MARKINGS
The aesthetics of a rain-bloated '70s fetish mag found in the woods.

CALL
They're for looking at, not listening to.

HABITAT
After-party VIP area at some guy's loft . . . heard he had drugs.

DIET
Pills and sexual harassment.

PREDATOR
See Party Crasher Photog, page 36.

SPOOR
Candid photos from "modeling sessions" will resurface in twenty years if they run for Congress.

THREATS
Suddenly realizing actions have consequences.

PORTFOLIO

STREET-LEVEL TREND-SPOTTER

If a trend gets enough press, it will create itself. Shaping culture into a parody of itself—one think-piece at a time.

MARKINGS
This new cultural signifier that, if you think about it, in a small way, captures the zeitgeist.

CALL
Just fill in: "[blank]-core"; "[blank]-punk."

HABITAT
Well-staked-out territory this species pretends to have just discovered.

DIET
Oh, only the hottest new style of cuisine that all the restos are lining up to offer.

BEHAVIOR
Find attention-seeking loner on the street doing something deviating from expectation—trend!

PREY
One Step Behind, page 37, the only group gullible enough to take their reportage as gospel when they eventually get around to reading it.

HOST SPECIES
Olds who want to know what the youngs are into (so they can dismiss or complain about it); weekend style sections that need filling.

All the celebs are doing it

The new hotness

Street snaps

For urban spelunking into abandoned schools to shout poignant photo essay that offsets visual soullessness

MOST POPULAR HAIRCUTS

UNDERCUT QUIFF

MODIFIED MCSQUEEB

GREASED SKRILLEX

INVERSE PATTERN
BALDNESS

POST PUBESCENT
BIEBER

BOARDWALK
IMPERIAL

HITLERJUGEND

THE R. KLOTZ

NEW NEW ORDER

PSEUDO RETRO BARBER

The Old Guard art of manliness is a ritual that requires the proper temple, and this species is the vestal virgin. Except they get laid, like, all the time.

MARKINGS
Marinating in blue-collar bravado to disguise the fact that their whole purpose is to make men look pretty and smell nice.

CALL
"I'm totally into the '50s thing except for the racism . . . and sexism . . . and constant threat of nuclear war, I guess."

HABITAT
Furnished in meticulously re-created old-fashioned detail . . . except with Wi-Fi.

DIET
Matching their clients shot-for-shot on free whiskey with a haircut offer; hand-rolled cigarettes; blue comb disinfectant if they're really jonesing.

SPOOR
Real authentic old-timey manly man macho fluffy; sandalwood-and-leather scent marking.

A classic shave needs an element of throat-slitting risk

There's a very personal and uninteresting meaning behind each tattoo

PARTY CRASHER PHOTOG

Maybe billing themselves as casual-wear CEOs or magazine portraitists, this species mainly wants to have a really great time all the time, no matter the fallout.

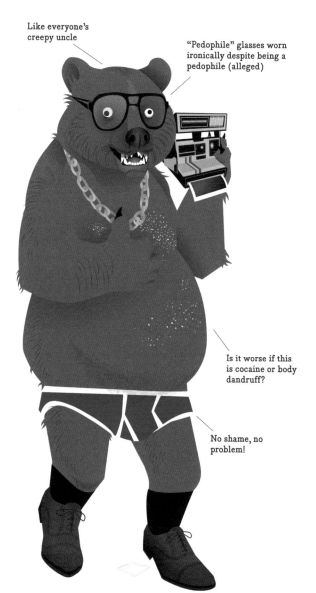

Like everyone's creepy uncle

"Pedophile" glasses worn ironically despite being a pedophile (alleged)

Is it worse if this is cocaine or body dandruff?

No shame, no problem!

MARKINGS
Why does he look so familiar? You saw his photo on a tabloid pleading "no contest" to groping a drunk 16-year-old.

CALL
"Come down to my studio sometime. We can have some wine and see what happens."

HABITAT
Parties where no one knows him but still mingling like a pro.

DIET
"Party snacks." (Cocaine.)

MATING
Always on the rut with a voracious appetite not hindered by petty matters of consent or decency.

BEHAVIOR
A gregarious nature yet other species are wary of their presence and find them off-putting.

CURRENTLY BARRED FROM ENTERING

IBIZA	REYKJAVÍK	GOA
AMSTERDAM	TEL AVIV	THAILAND (ALL OF IT)
DUBAI	VATICAN CITY	

ONE STEP BEHIND

Am I cool yet?

MARKINGS
Whatever everyone was into, like, forever ago.

CALL
Quoting something you're, like, totally over.

HABITAT
The hazy twilight between things that are really trendy right now and things that are so uncool you can pretend to like them for a laugh.

DIET
Bacon! Bacon everything! (Obsessing over bacon is hilarious.)

BEHAVIOR
Icing; planking; Harlem-shaking.

PREDATORS
On-trend mean girls eye rolling and snickering while doling out false compliments.

THREATS
Eventual dawn of self-awareness; crushing embarrassment.

Trucker hat (2003)

Shutter shades (2007)

Keffiyeh (2000–2005)

Three wolf moon shirt (2009)

Huge cuffs on selvedge denim (2001)

FESTIFEST!

The sun is out (where applicable), the temperature is tolerable . . . all signs point to FESTIVAL!, a nomadic bazaar of creatives offering their labors of love. With elements cribbed from a religious procession, a taking-peyote-in-the desert weekend festival, and a Christmas white-elephant market, the "festival" never fully defines itself.

Neighborhoods that pride themselves on being home to a particular counterculture artistic spark ("staying weird") must publicly declare it in the form of a parade/festival/fair at least once a year or lose their quirk accreditation. Many examples of such were begun years or decades earlier by the artists who first dared gentrify the burnt-out husk of urban decay where the neighborhood stands and now have devolved into a ritualistic set of traditions with little sense of their original meaning.

THE BAZAAR

The standing army of the creative assault is a paragon of capitalism in the cloak of individual self-expression. The merchants encamped and the wares they offer may include the following:

* ★ "Suzy homemaker" home-sewn retro-kitsch aprons (doesn't know how to make anything else)
* ★ Designer "dresses" that you can drape "hundreds of ways" because they're just squares of stretch jersey with holes cut in them
* ★ Guy who sells tube socks who didn't research demographics
* ★ Earnest recruiter for wind farm/legalized marijuana/outsider candidate for position no one cares about campaign
* ★ Giclée prints of high school art class–quality whimsy (hot air balloons/bikes/octopodes)

* ★ Pop culture idols crudely stenciled onto thrifted paintings
* ★ Jewelry made from reclaimed clock parts/bike chains/medical waste
* ★ Vinyl records melted into bowls
* ★ JV trophies upcycled into door knobs/bookends/sex toys
* ★ Hardback books, gutted and filled with blank paper, never to actually be used
* ★ Bales of lavender, absolute masses of it
* ★ Homemade soap (up to ten booths)
* ★ Wafts of stink bud + grilled meat smell

I ♥ A PARADE

The mobile artillery of the offensive, the parade is usually a celebration of a
not-actually-a-holiday holiday. Tongue-in-cheek bacchanalia to shock the squares?
A tribute to ensconced rights of public gathering? All good enough . . . let's
get our march on with . . .

nude marchers in melting body paint	divorced dad in bushwacker hat	bikes with too many wheels	bikes with not enough wheels	bikes ridden by nudes in melting body paint
papier mache vagina on a stick	perambulating attention seeker	terrified-looking pet on someone's head	big creepy puppet operated by 10-12 stoners	celebrity spotting: a one-hit band member
celebrity spotting: out of work indie film actor	street philosopher publishing in chalk-on-pavement media	N	traumatized child witness	ambiguous counter-protest
lewd act in broad daylight	aggressively friendly clipboarder running interference	pseudo-pagan "ritual" of no fixed mythology	a painful sunburn in an unfortunate place	conspicuous undercover cop, not fooling anyone
gray-ponytailed throwback in button-encrusted army jacket	post-dichotomous omnigender baton/flag twirling squad	mermaid in a wheelchair	miasma of aerosolized body glitter	rival anarchist brass bands playing over each other

TECH & ONLINE

APPLE UPDATE EARLY ADOPTER

Before everyone else even considered a Mac product or an iGadget, this species had leaked it, preordered it, bought it, unboxed it, reboxed it, and shot a video of re-unboxing it, reviewed it, debated it, defended it, gotten into a flame war for it, updated it, cracked it, broke it, fixed it, and traded it up for the newer model.

MARKINGS
Cultivates the sangfroid of a staircase made of reinforced glass: an Apple Store come to life.

CALL
The sound of clicking "yes" on every permission pop-up.

HABITAT
Betwixt rounded corners, matte steel, beveled edges, and drop reflections.

DIET
DL release rumors.

MATING
Achieves climax watching livestream of CEO announcing new consumer products.

BEHAVIOR
Clocks the moments of their lives by iTunes updates.

PREDATOR
Android (both the phone platform and actual killer robots).

THREATS
Having to defend the use of sweatshop labor; realizing brand is coasting on reputation rather than innovation; Flash compatibility.

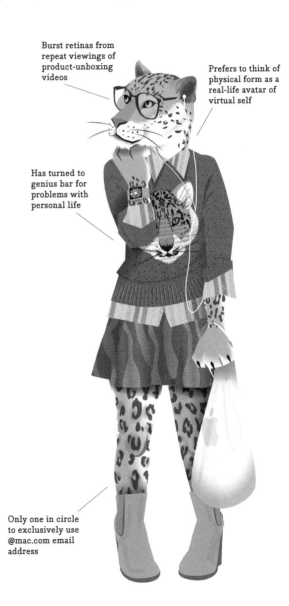

Burst retinas from repeat viewings of product-unboxing videos

Prefers to think of physical form as a real-life avatar of virtual self

Has turned to genius bar for problems with personal life

Only one in circle to exclusively use @mac.com email address

WEB SERIES LINE PRODUCER

The Internet as entertainment platform has opened up whole new arenas for hopeful video auteurs with big ideas and no budget. This species acts as middle managers, facilitating their dream by doing all the grunt work.

Needs 100 extras 8 a.m. Sunday. No $—but great experience & exposure!

Ends up holding the boom mic because no one else wants to

Only one who came on time to the shoot

MARKINGS
A weary, put-upon brow; easily-taken-advantage-of manner.

CALL
"Do you have an office we can shoot in for 11 hours? Anyone? Just a regular office. I'm *desperate!*"

HABITAT
Crowd-sourcing sites—hourly hitting "refresh" on the donation total page.

DIET
There's no money for craft service; everyone has to bring their own snacks.

PREDATORS
Advantage-taking director friends with no organizational skills; every barely legal development supervisor of media corps' "online media division" who never met an exploitative rights contract they didn't like.

SEE ALSO
Particularly resentful of Internet Celebrity, page 49, for virality without effort.

SOCIAL MEDIA BRANDING NETWORK ANALYST OR WHATEVER

Meh. The world is meh. Everything is meh.

MARKINGS
Meh.

CALL
Meh.

HABITAT
Meh.

DIET
Meh.

RANGE
Meh.

SPOOR
Meh.

NEST
Meh.

MATING
Meh.

THREATS
Meh.

PREDATORS
Meh.

Meh

Meh

Meh

Meh

MOBILE APP BROGRAMMER

Also known as a dynamic solutions architect, idea dreamgineer, or some variation on "___ rock star" or "___ ninja" despite being a master of neither the guitar nor shinobi-no-jutsu.

Blue sky

Cloud based

Next wave

MARKINGS
The latest in wearables; seemingly limitless self-confidence based on nothing.

CALL
"Just popcorn out your thoughts, guys!"; "Let me piggyback off of your idea . . . What if [repeats idea near verbatim]."

HABITAT
"Disruptive" open-plan offices; "game-changing" TED Talks; formerly poor "iconic" neighborhoods now pricing out their residents.

DIET
"Revolutionary," "innovative," "lifestyle-integrated" power bars.

THREATS
Anyone realizing that he has no idea what he's talking about; tech bubble bursts.

FUN FACTS
In larval stage, prey for larger species; as adult, aggressive predator of same species/anyone else in proximity.

SOCIAL NETWORK "FRIEND"

? THIS BOOK DOES NOT HAVE EMOJI SUPPORT ?

MARKINGS
[heart] [heart] [heart] [cell phone]
[heart] [heart] [heart]

CALL
[eggplant] [conical pile of crap
with googly eyes] [hand pointing]
[interrobang]

HABITAT
[toilet] [flamenco dancer] [Mt. Fuji]
[toilet]

DIET
[pizza] [pizza] [pizza] [cigarette]
[mushroom cloud]

THREATS
[knife] [gun] [bomb] [dragon]
[crying face] [violin]

SPOOR
[blue square] [red square] [blue
square] [red square]

WARNING
[snow cone] [clapping hands] [snow
cone] [clapping hands] [inscrutable
Japanese thing]

¯_(?)_/¯

[phone emoji]

[winky/tongue emoji]

[key emoji]

[shoe emoji]

STILL-COOL DADDY BLOGGER

The significant other works; he doesn't want to. That's not laziness, it's progressive. More time to bond with the kiddo but still pursue all those great creative projects of his bachelor days.

Training the next generation. . . junior's the scene queen of playgroup

A couple of gens old. This one's the baby's; I got two other ones

Doesn't understand object permanence, but up on Joey, Johnny, Dee Dee, Tommy, and Marky's contribution to popular music

MARKINGS
Trendier dresser than anyone else in his mommy meet-up group, despite the applesauce blowback.

CALL
"Mason! Olive! Otto! Quinn!"

HABITAT
Bench near the playground, eyes glued to music blog on the smartphone; happy hour in his local bar as his kid runs riot ("It takes a village of day drunks to raise a child, man.").

DIET
Whatever's left of the kid's mucus-slicked goji-flaxseed cookie.

THREATS
Mommy bloggers who hog all the free gimmes to "product review"; when's Daddy gonna get a taste?

SPOOR
In his spare moments runs a glossy mag called something twee like *Kitestring* or *Juicebox Quarterly* full of photoshoots of other cool dads in high-ceilinged brownstones. A single issue costs more than a humanely raised aged steak.

INSTAGRAM NARCISSIST

A picture is worth a thousand words, so this species' output outranks The Odyssey, The Iliad, the Bible, and Stephen King's entire Dark Tower series combined.

MARKINGS

Not much to look at but always looking at everything else; the one with a camera phone screen permanently glued to their eye socket.

CALL

(shutter click.)

HABITAT

Anywhere there are things to see, document, upload, comment on, and "like."

DIET

Snaps every meal before eating; if social niceties allowed it, would also photograph when it came out the other end, too.

MATING

Heavily and intimately recorded; revenge-leaked after breakup.

NEST

In physical world, spare. On "inspiration file" digital pinboard, lavishly furnished and littered with conversation pieces.

THREATS

Forced to experience life in real time rather than capturing it for future playback.

Found this great tutorial on new ways to tie headscarves and made a how-to step-by-step photo post to share

Had about 50 thumbnails of ponchos bookmarked before finding "the one"

Like!

CLICKBAIT ANGLER

Mad click-throughs. Total social engagement. No actual content.

Only '90s Kids Will Totally Get This War!

We will never reach Peak Kitten-Falling-Off-a-Couch

16 Bags That Think They're People! (click for slideshow)

MARKINGS
NEW MIRACLE CURE for filling the workday with mindless lowest common denominator reptile brain triggers.

HABITAT
YOU WON'T BELIEVE WHAT HAPPENS NEXT when an English literature major can't find any other work and signs on to a brain-dead online content farm.

CALL
DOCTORS HATE HER FOR communicating entirely through animated GIFs of retro TV double-takes.

DIET
MAKES $$$ WORKING IN HER SPARE TIME through amalgamated click-throughs, video views, retweets . . . YUM!

PREY
THIS ONE WEIRD TRICK only exploits the interests of a particularly intellectually incurious 18–25-year-old demographic!!!!

BUZZ-WANK QUIZZES

TITS OR KITTENS?

WHICH BRANDED CONTENT ARE YOU?

HOW MANY TIMES CAN YOU CLICK THIS?

WHICH LOLS ARE ROTFL?!

INTERNET CELEBRITY

Contemporary culture is so obsessed with celebrities that sometimes there aren't enough from established sources to go around. Luckily, the Internet comes to the rescue with unintimidating figures not necessarily possessing talent or ability or achievements but accessible to anyone with Ethernet access.

MARKINGS
Nonthreateningly attractive to the emerging sexuality of tweens; slightly too ugly to be in a boy band/star in a tween sitcom.

CALL
Vague encouraging advice about being true to yourself/following your dreams; unfunny jokes; fart noises.

HABITAT
"Trending" list on social networks; pulling goofy faces (but totally crushable) in front of a webcam.

DIET
Attention. Starved for it.

FUN FACT
Ask younger sibling or cousin to confirm identity; invisible and unknown to anyone of legal drinking age.

LIFE CYCLE
If still attractive upon maturity, this species pupates into Immersive ~~Theater~~ Theatre Auteur, page 95; the rest become the submissive Web Series Line Producer, page 42, or Film Festival Rejectee, page 75.

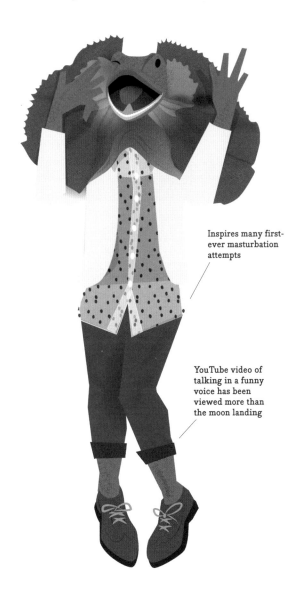

Inspires many first-ever masturbation attempts

YouTube video of talking in a funny voice has been viewed more than the moon landing

140 CARICATURE

Specially adapted to convey the day-to-day essence of life in sporadic micro-bursts, so less is more, but more often.

MARKINGS
One appendage always on a text-emitting device.

CALL
Mimetic responses to top trending #hashtag game prompt "substitute arbitrary nouns for other noun in title"

HABITAT
Wherever the 4G gets more bars.

DIET
Whatever it is, they will be sure to fully describe it over several dozen rapid-fire posts with more detail than you ever cared to know.

BEHAVIOR
Determines the day's activities based on what's going to flow best in 140 character bursts.

SPOOR
Moment-by-moment log of every fleeting thought.

THREATS
Mass unfollowings.

Hasn't met their closest friends in three dimensions

#hashtag

WHY WE TWEET

"Liveblogging a major sporting event or award show is a great feeling of community—we're united by bitching about how much it sucks."

"I can unload unfocused rage and threats on strangers without all the hassle of lighting bags on doorsteps."

"I bought 10,000 followers to try and get a book deal. I'll buy 10,000 people to read my book."

"I stole the name of a famous comedian and post jokes stolen from other comedians' accounts. Am I famous yet?"

"I can connect with all my favorite brands and trick their media intern into saying something that will cause a PR shitstorm!"

"Microblogging is just a transitional stage. I'm already honing my thoughts down to 10-15 characters for fermiblogging."

THE FOLLOWED
(3000+)

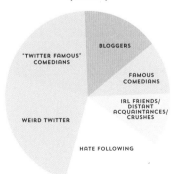

- BLOGGERS
- "TWITTER FAMOUS" COMEDIANS
- FAMOUS COMEDIANS
- IRL FRIENDS/ DISTANT ACQUAINTANCES/ CRUSHES
- WEIRD TWITTER
- HATE FOLLOWING

WHO FOLLOWS THE FOLLOWER
(X< 500)

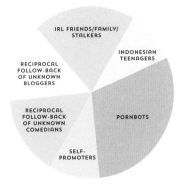

- IRL FRIENDS/FAMILY/ STALKERS
- INDONESIAN TEENAGERS
- RECIPROCAL FOLLOW-BACK OF UNKNOWN BLOGGERS
- PORNBOTS
- RECIPROCAL FOLLOW-BACK OF UNKNOWN COMEDIANS
- SELF-PROMOTERS

MUSIC

LEAD UKULELE IN GANGSTA RAP COVER BAND

Who could have guessed that the anguished anthems of the disenfranchised underclass would one day be trivialized into aggressive whimsy by college kids? I mean, aside from anyone with a passing familiarity of American popular music of the last 200 years.

MARKINGS
Aggressive prints; bright colors; themed costumes.

CALL
Plinky tuning; faux gang signs; undermining of earlier generation's anthems of anger and protest.

HABITAT
Sharing the bar's lineup with an improv troupe, a comedian, and an "erotic" magic act; on soundtracks of ads for lifestyle products to convey earnestness.

DIET
Like an unsupervised five-year-old at a birthday party.

BEHAVIOR
Intentional off-putting weirdness that masks social inadequacy; giggling at non-jokes.

PREY
Less confident misfits in awe of this species' ability to hold eye contact with strangers.

FUN FACT
Landed on this after trying circus arts, pie making, and podcasting.

If you're going to play a toy instrument, you've got to dress like a child

Thinks their "can't sing, can't play" technique comes off as charming

♫ The 1-8-7 don't stop, on undercover cops ♫

Shuffling off-kilter dance

BAND (CONDENSED)

Not a DJ. But still kind of a DJ.

Automatically
synchronizing
cardinal grammeter

MARKINGS
If ugly/French, adopts a mechanical/
oversized head that obscures all
facial features as visual signature.

CALL
Mathematically based electronic
streams that technically count as
"music."

HABITAT
On stage twiddling knobs in a
way that technically counts as
"performance."

DIET
E-cigarettes; well drinks.

HOST SPECIES
Equally introverted dance-floor
nodders.

FUN FACT
All their electronic equipment weighs
as much as a traditional four-piece
rock combo!

Six hydrocoptic
marzlevanes

Forescent skor novertrunnion

Shoe

'80S NITE KARAOKE STAR

Uses quirk, self-assurance, and dramatic overestimation of their vocal range to ruthlessly prey on the audience's patience.

MARKINGS
Always wears the boa, funny glasses, and piano-key tie provided as stage props and can pull them off with grace.

CALL
Power ballad to the people!

HABITAT
No private rooms; gotta be the big bar stage. Even better with a live band.

DIET
Big meaty riffs; cheesy love lyrics; Meat Loaf.

MATING
Looks deep into potential mate's eyes and sings "Almost Paradise" directly to them.

THREATS
Being shown up by rivals who can switch between English and German on "99 Luftballons" without even looking at the monitor.

BEHAVIOR
A wacky sidekick in search of a sitcom; mic hogging.

FUN FACT
Acutely suffers from high school drama club/chorus withdrawal.

The target audience for all jukebox musicals

Nostalgic for "I heart the '80s" nostalgia

Unaware that all favorite "'80s songs" came out in the early '90s

Entire concept of American culture between 1979 and 1990 = Day-Glo

New Jack Swingin'

FESTIVAL QUEUE-CUTTER

Quick to identify their special status by waving their press pass like a cross against vampires.

Secretly scanning others' badges to see what blogs they're with and if they got better access

Furiously texting PR rep after getting stopped at securtiy

Military surplus gives touch of fuck-the-Man, even at the Poland Spring™ This Is Refreshment® Tomorrow-ventions® Mainstage by Cadillac™

Festival semi-nudity is for day-trippers and hack actresses

MARKINGS
Moldering wristbands from festivals previous kept on for sentimental reasons/bragging rights.

CALL
Sniffy comparisons of current fest and crowd in attendance to previous years.

HABITAT
Review blog named for unreleased Neutral Milk Hotel track.

PREDATOR
Those who call out their bullshit in front of security.

THREATS
Actual/thoughtful/respected music writing.

PREY
Easily impressed undergrad music majors with open bar tabs.

MATING
Unhealthy obsession with hot new band's hot new drummer; refers to her as "a young Kim Gordon" in an otherwise scathing review.

BEHAVIOR
Standing awkwardly in VIP area, then, immediately dropping everything to follow headliner for 20 feet as they walk into the *actual* VIP area.

THE OPENING ACT'S OPENING ACT

Electronic bleep-bloop dance sounds are fine, but every generation needs to rock out. For a bit. Until the next software upgrade comes out.

MARKINGS
Okay-looking but definitely needs the "I'm in a band" card to get laid.

CALL
Way, way too much stage banter.

HABITAT
"The green room" = maintenance hallway.

DIET
Drink tickets.

NEST
Sleeps in the practice space since boyfriend/girlfriend kicked 'em out; insulated with a thick layer of broken-down guitars, odd percussion instruments, and empty beer bottles.

SPOOR
Only merch for sale is hand-labeled CDs burned on home computer and single white undershirt with band name and tour dates (both of them) written in permanent marker.

HOST SPECIES
The venue's booker who owes a favor.

PREY
Two teenagers at their first concert ever in empty venue who took the "doors open" time seriously.

Still struggling with nailing that third chord

Not sure if it's cool yet to advocate for a rediscovery of Don Henley's solo work

cull.

JAM FOR FRANCES

Sound board operator using this set to check levels for opening act

Considers this gig "putting in dues"

NEOFOLK BUSKER

In a digital area of slickness and perfection, a true rebel revives the old days when everything was shit.

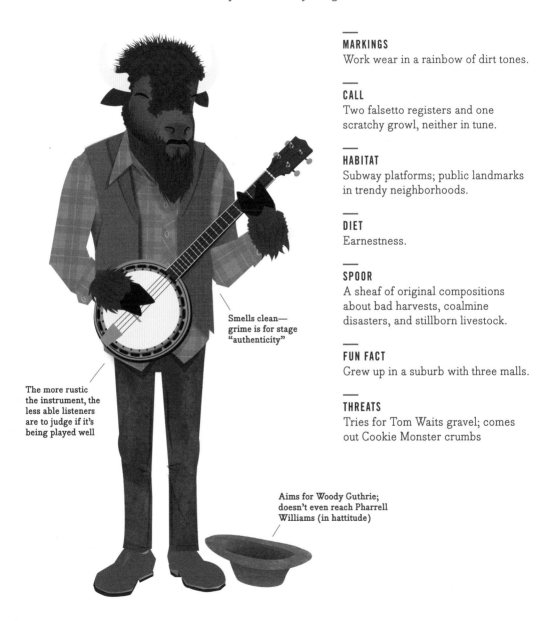

MARKINGS
Work wear in a rainbow of dirt tones.

CALL
Two falsetto registers and one scratchy growl, neither in tune.

HABITAT
Subway platforms; public landmarks in trendy neighborhoods.

DIET
Earnestness.

SPOOR
A sheaf of original compositions about bad harvests, coalmine disasters, and stillborn livestock.

FUN FACT
Grew up in a suburb with three malls.

THREATS
Tries for Tom Waits gravel; comes out Cookie Monster crumbs

Smells clean—grime is for stage "authenticity"

The more rustic the instrument, the less able listeners are to judge if it's being played well

Aims for Woody Guthrie; doesn't even reach Pharrell Williams (in hattitude)

OH NO! I LEFT THE HOUSE WITHOUT MY TATTOOS.

HOW EMBARRASSING!

CAN YOU DRAW ME SOME NEW ONES?

O PIONEERS!

A GENTRIFICATION CYCLE

The Neighborhood was once the busy home to unionized blue-collar workers and family-owned shops, full of sturdy brownstones and no-frills tenements. The belt rusted. The union busted. The riots rioted. Now it barely hangs on at the intersection of urban blight and industrial decay.

The first homesteaders—artsy, unconventional, and short of cash—acquire abandoned oversized space for pennies on the dollar and avoid overt street crime, sidewalks littered with bodies of comatose junkies and flash-frozen homeless, and food deserts. The Neighborhood overflows with untapped potential. The recent transplants (the conscious ones, at least) are friendly and deferential to their downwardly mobile neighbors, but everyone knows where this is headed.

Hearing boasts of this "undiscovered gem" (which leave out the rampant robbery/homelessness), like-minded individuals take up the cause and relocate. Finally, a decent restaurant opens in a former methadone clinic, followed by an organic bodega. Groceries no longer have to be carried in from other boroughs. Cabs start agreeing to come to the Neighborhood after dark.

The Neighborhood becomes a destination for food, drink, and good times. Rents rise 200 percent. The original homesteaders begin to feel old, complain about changes, and wax nostalgic for the junkies and mugging. It becomes a true mark of trendiness to be a full-time resident. Students, hangers-on, and wannabes flood the Neighborhood. Real bank branches open in former payday-loan storefronts. The area boasts multiple bold restaurants and indie boutiques. Original downwardly mobile residents are strong-armed out by landlords with dollar signs for eyes.

The Neighborhood name is now shorthand for *hip* and well known enough to be parodied in memes of the day. The newspaper of record (that only squares and old people read) recognizes the revival of the formerly abandoned hellscape.

Rents rise 500 percent. National chains open in the Neighborhood; construction begins on "luxury condos."

An unsustainable glut of frozen yogurterias all inexplicably open at the same time and then go out of business (a blip).

Rents rise 1,000 percent. The Neighborhood is now insufferable. Most storefronts are now bank branches. Original keystone bar that reinvented the Neighborhood is forced to close, becomes a bank branch. Original pioneers can no longer afford to live here but were thinking of having kids anyway so move to new abandoned neighborhood for more space. Their lofts are torn down to make room for more bank branches. The last economically disadvantaged resident dies after being run over by a moving van.

The stereotype of the gentrifying is cemented in pop culture's mind, contrary to the evolving reality and association with a past time (first nostalgically, then dismissively). The generations shift. Middle-aged writers who've never been to the Neighborhood write the mockable stereotype into network sitcoms. The only people clueless enough to still buy into the Neighborhood's cool reputation are tourists and sixteen-year-old girls on the Internet from somewhere else.

The local university builds monolithic, depressing dorms. Students from the suburbs move in among the national chains and bank branches and don't know what once was. Landlords are unable to fill the expensive luxury condos in the neighborhood of bank branches, and former yogurterias become drug addicts and lay unconscious on sidewalks. The Neighborhood returns to decay for the next twenty years.

Will the cycle repeat?

FRIENDS & LOVERS

WEED DELIVERY GUY

Nothing to see here, officer.

CALL
Quick to point out how *Breaking Bad* totally got it all wrong but has never stocked anything stronger than hash.

HABITAT
Your doorstep in 15 minutes.

DIET
This girl I know does killer edibles.

SPOOR
Recently moved from bags to colored acrylic boxes—in a digital age it's essential to appreciate the beauty of "the object."

PREY
New-to-the-city kiddies who got the number from their older cousin who won't notice they just paid $20 for an ounce of oregano.

THREATS
Loneliness . . . Why does everyone just go to the dispensary now instead of calling for drugs? Is it because I kept a pager for so long?

FUN FACT
With the decriminalization of marijuana, this species is critically endangered from habitat loss. Sorry, this fact isn't really "fun" per se.

When pot goes legal, loses appeal of risk and becomes just a smelly delivery guy

Use our app for GPS-targeted delivery in one of our branded mini-cars with signature red-rimmed, dazed-looking headlights

Yes! Will accept your University Meal Plan Flexible Spending card

WAY-TOO-SEX-POSITIVE CRUSADER

This species firmly believes that the Sexual Revolution didn't go far enough because it wasn't as successful as that old French one. (Nothing is hotter than being GGG for guillotine-play, BTW.) If the free-love movement did a little more beheading, all public gatherings would end with an orgy and the handjob would have replaced the handshake.

Full of wacky anecdotes about misunderstanding between various polyamorous partners

Ready to argue merits of water-based lube versus organic coconut oil anytime!

In an "open relationship" with appropriate social niceties

MARKINGS
Treats her jacket lapels like a conspiracy theorist's car bumper: all the stances up front.

CALL
Chatty, approachable, careful about pronouns; can work "G-spot" into any conversation.

HABITAT
"Friendly" dildo 'n' vibe stores that offer "workshops" and "readings."

DIET
(Gratuitous innuendo here.)

BEHAVIOR
Blames a sex-fearing society when asked to leave brunch for loudly describing the features of butt plugs with demonstrative hand gestures.

MATING
Yes, please.

THREATS
Media conglomerate owners clear-cutting the free weeklies' sex columns.

SEE ALSO
Stand-Up Storyteller, page 73, with oversharing stories no one really wants to hear.

SPAZZY PUCKISH CRUSH GIRL

Long imagined in works of fiction composed by sexually frustrated male auteurs, this species is a far rarer sight in most real-world settings.

MARKINGS
A charming feminine mishmash of styles that seems effortless; unsullied vulnerability; "goofy" faces that are still attractive.

HABITAT
Debut novels and short films by sexually frustrated writers (see The Hot Literary Prospect, page 101).

NEST
Openly displays her prescription bottles as trophies of her specialness.

CALL
Vocalizations of childlike wonder; affirming platitudes; overtly expressed love of life.

MATING
Initiates copulation by shaking up staid protagonist's ordered lifestyle; hyperactive whimsy ensues.

THREATS
Expressing natural agency; showing more dimensions.

Affects only the "cute," fun kinds of mental illness, not the messy, sad ones

Overawed by the beauty of living and wants to share it with *you*

Quirky, but not *too* quirky; mismatched, but not *too* mismatched

REGRETTABLE ONE-NIGHT STAND

Really? What were you thinking?

Ugh, just get over yourself. You're not that hot.

Trying so hard to come off fun and quirky. Give it a rest.

Some band he won't shut up about because he knows the drummer.

Eh, hold on to his number in case of a dry spell. You've done worse.

MARKINGS
Online profile had all the right bands; a good photo.

CALL
hey :) (via text)

HABITAT
Smartphone dating app; dive bar at last call; in your memoir chapter titled "Why?"

DIET
Your body, baby. All. Night. Long.

SPOOR
There isn't enough penicillin in the world to deal with the living Petri dish of STDs inside him.

BEHAVIOR
Everything that seemed charmingly free-spirited the night before is annoying in daylight.

FUN FACT
They're not even that good a lay.

THE INTERNET BLIND DATE

Despite the density and "walkability" of your environs, just bumping into a future mate without forethought is unlikely, so you end up meeting this species whether you want to or not.

CALL
Too many details about the ex but brags about knowing the difference between their, there, and they're.

HABITAT
A well-lit public place.

DIET
Just a no-pressure drink. Let's not put labels on anything yet.

RANGE
Age 21–32 (but actually 42).

NEST
Feathered with namechecks to the right bands, right TV dramas, and right tone of knowing self-deprecation.

PREDATORS
Trolls dive-bombing with e–sexual harassment, a dick pic, and a smiley face.

THREATS
Getting swiped past for the clichéd photo at Machu Picchu while her snarky profile goes unread.

SPOOR
Increasingly desperate after-date text messages left unreturned.

Looking for a "partner in crime" to go on "crazy adventures" with

I'm "laid-back." So laid-back, but also "easygoing." But I still "go for it!"

Definitely shorter than they said they were; fatter, too

Smokes only when drinking; vegetarian, but only when drinking

Ugh! Stop asking for pictures of my feet

MOOCHER ON YOUR COUCH

... FOR THE NEXT SIX MONTHS. EIGHT MAX, I PROMISE.

A modern nomad living each day as it comes, ready for whatever adventure fate throws their way, free to. . . Are you going to finish that?

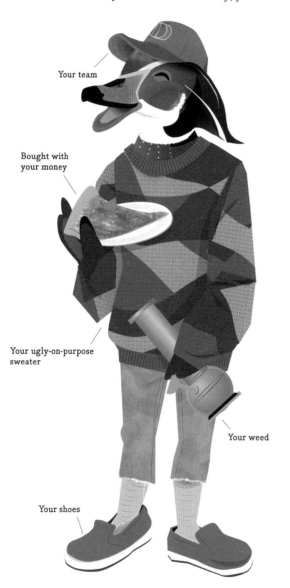

Your team

Bought with your money

Your ugly-on-purpose sweater

Your weed

Your shoes

MARKINGS
Unburdened by modern life's possessions and schedules, frequently burdened by your possessions.

CALL
(stoned giggling)

HABITAT
Cities with rents they couldn't possibly afford; towns near colleges they couldn't possibly have gotten into.

DIET
Beer, burritos, whatever you left in the fridge/garbage.

HOST SPECIES
Females with absentee/alcoholic fathers; pathologically unassertive males.

FUN FACT
This species has unique senses unable to detect social cues or strained politeness.

YOUR COFFEE SHOP CRUSH

Sure, a flirty barista is a cliché, but it didn't come out of nowhere.

MARKINGS
Totally cute but also really approachable and not stuck up at all.

CALL
"I'm just doing this for beer money until [nebulous other career] takes off, y'know."

HABITAT
At the corner café that isn't even the best one in the neighborhood but you made it your regular.

MATING
Didn't mention a partner in brief exchange at the register so maaaaaybe is available?

BEHAVIOR
Bumping and grinding the milk steamer in time to the drum and bass playing on the café's turntable.

SPOOR
Impressive latte art . . . sculpts a vulva in the foam of your macchiato.

HOST SPECIES
Love-struck but tongue-tied patrons who communicate affection through tip jar.

FUN FACT
Not actually into you. Sorry not sorry.

Doesn't really actually care much about coffee, but the bosses are cool and let her come in late

Raises just ever so slightly and shows the tiniest flash of skin when reaching for the beans on the high shelf

ENTERTAINMENT & RECREATION

OUTDOOR SCREENING HECKLER

The silver screen was once a communal experience, as was drunken nature worship. The phenomenon of the parkside or rooftop movie screening fuses the two, and this species ruins it for everyone.

MARKINGS
Somehow got grass stains on their tongue.

CALL
"THAT'S WHAT SHE SAID!"; "FUCK YOOOOOOOUUUUU!"; "WHAT IS REALITY!?"

HABITAT
Screenings of beloved classics or experimental short films in parks/on rooftops (seasonal); migrates indoors to shout at open mics in cold weather.

DIET
Been hammering micheladas since the onscreen HBO logo flew into outer space/the MGM lion roared.

BEHAVIOR
One-person *Rocky Horror* Audience Participation Machine (the movie showing is not *RHPS*).

THREATS
Eye rolls from fellow moviegoers; a flying beer bottle to the head by the third act.

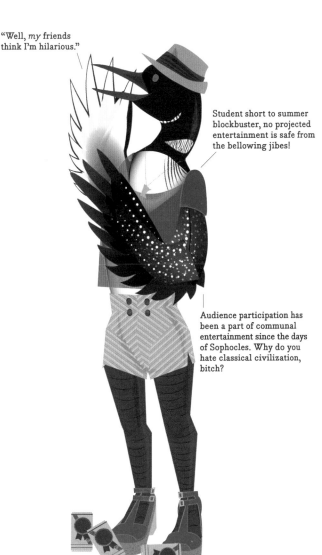

"Well, *my* friends think I'm hilarious."

Student short to summer blockbuster, no projected entertainment is safe from the bellowing jibes!

Audience participation has been a part of communal entertainment since the days of Sophocles. Why do you hate classical civilization, bitch?

EMPOWERED BURLY-CUTIE

*Juxtaposing overtly sexual displays with the least sexy scraps of pop culture—*Twin Peaks' Log Lady, It's Pat, *the writing of Ayn Rand, and so on—this species transforms cheap arousal into social commentary and weapons of self-esteem.*

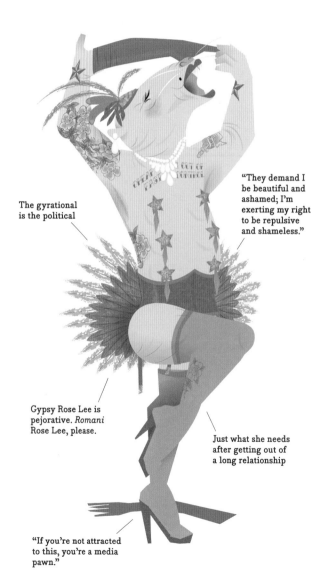

The gyrational is the political

"They demand I be beautiful and ashamed; I'm exerting my right to be repulsive and shameless."

Gypsy Rose Lee is pejorative. *Romani* Rose Lee, please.

Just what she needs after getting out of a long relationship

"If you're not attracted to this, you're a media pawn."

MARKINGS
Looks fully clothed when naked and viewed from behind due to tessellating tattoos on 85% of skin surface.

CALL
"If Marilyn Monroe were alive today, she'd be a size 57 and weigh 400 pounds. She'd need to be lifted out of her house with a crane. Think about *that*."

HABITAT
The too-small stage of a dingy dive on a slow weeknight; cable access.

DIET
Anything they want. Dieting is a conspiracy to redirect sensual desire into self-loathing.

THREATS
The non-ironic unaware cis male gaze.

SPOOR
Unfettered distribution of crotch sweat on all backstage seating options.

BEHAVIOR
Unsettling amount of winking

STAND-UP STORYTELLER

While traumatic stories are usually retold on the therapist's couch or blurted out on a blind date to fill an awkward silence, this species spins yarns into gold as a personal industry of cashing in on their own misfortune.

MARKINGS
Lovably rumpled, lending immediate relatability to audience.

CALL
Best-case scenario: a rambling tale of gay bed-hopping and bottomed-out meth benders; more likely: a sob story about being peed on at summer camp.

HABITAT
Crazy scrapes of improbable circumstances blindly wandered into.

DIET
Bottled water, nervously swigged on stage mid-story to indicate a transition in the narrative.

SPOOR
Desperately pitched collection of personal essays to any publisher with an email address.

THREATS
Sober audiences; the flashing red light signaling time's up.

SUBSPECIES
- Writers with great stories who are terrible public speakers
- Stage-savvy actors with nothing interesting to talk about

Too ugly to be an actor; too unfunny to be a comic

Confessional vulnerability

Quirky or just color-blind?

COMEDY SCENE DORK

Those who can't do, teach. Those who can't do either become super-fans. This species wraps its raison d'être in what it loves but can't do itself, creating a fallacy that it is contributing to the environment it only passively observes.

Slowly alienates entire peer group with a barrage of invites to open mics and improv jams in bar basements

Tithes 10 to 40% of income to improv workshops and coaches

Doesn't actually have a sense of humor but enjoys being humor-adjacent

The *Lampoon* rejected all their submissions

MARKINGS
Identifies self with knowing nod and smug facial expression to show they "get it."

CALL
Applying basic comedy structure guidelines to all areas of life; someone else's satirical observations retold badly.

HABITAT
So many podcasts.

DIET
Needs five or six beers to get the courage to shout suggestions for the improv set.

LIFE CYCLE
Like elephants to their graveyard, inevitably migrates to Los Angeles after being pushed out of East Coast/ Midwest by younger, more camera-ready rivals.

THREATS
Afraid of girls; if female, afraid of self.

FILM FESTIVAL REJECTEE

Film is dead. This species is prying the gold fillings out of the corpse's teeth.

MARKINGS
Carries film festival tote bag everywhere.

CALL
Denouncing film criticism as bullshit, except for maybe Pauline Kael's stuff about Scorsese, but she hated *Star Wars*, so fuck her.

HABITAT
Local Wi-Fi coffee shop. Nine hours a day of writing time for the price of one small iced coffee and some death stares from baristas.

BEHAVIOR
Wants to be the Wes Anderson of his generation by making films exactly like Wes Anderson but slightly worse.

SPOOR
Films that aren't *safe* enough for those corporate stooges at [insert any festival], I guess.

SUBSPECIES
Close kin with all documentary-dabblers—all you need these days is the right marginal '80s cultural phenomenon and enough obsessive weirdos to do the talking-head stuff.

THREATS
Manager of local art-house movie theater refusing to give professional-courtesy discount.

Convinced that *smart* audiences will see past film's production value lapses to greater "ideas" beneath

Because digital lacks warmth

Continuity problem? Fill in the gaps with slick, minimal animated sequences

HUNGOVER YOGI

All beings on this physical plane are limited by mortality and the suffering of attachment. This species, while dedicated to spiritual and flexible betterment, believes if suffering is inevitable, at least they're going to have a good time the night before.

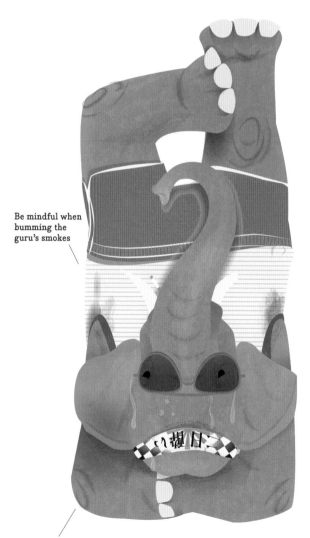

Be mindful when bumming the guru's smokes

Toxins (aka last night's 15 Moscow mules) sweating out of system

MARKINGS
Bloodshot third eye; clammy chakras; tantric regret.

CALL
Repeating mantra: "Liquorbeforebeerneverfear . . ."

HABITAT
Low-down dives with legendarily apocalyptic bathrooms; after-hours lounges where narcotics are sold openly; marauding caravans of like-minded substance abusers wandering the streets in search of the next big score . . . and yoga class once a week.

DIET
Greasy namastakeout.

BEHAVIOR
Self-actualization (pushing to the front of bar line); spreading peace (buying rounds); allowing life energy to flow freely (vomiting in gutters).

MORNING-AFTER ASANAS

TOO-BRIGHT-IN-HERE SUN SALUTATION
OHM MY ACHING BACK
DOWNWARD-FACING CHUNDER
I-WISH-I-WAS-DEAD SAVASANA

BEER LEAGUE BOCCE CHAMP

In times of olde, rivals would struggle for dominance through direct combat. Still having that need to show mastery over upstarts, this species channels competitiveness into what seems to outsiders to be a silly, elder-aping distraction.

MARKINGS
More expensive uniforms than most triple-A teams.

CALL
Running under-breath sports-radio-cliché-filled commentary done in weak impression of broadcasting legend (such as Harry Caray, Dick Vitale, or Sid Waddell if you're nasty).

HABITAT
Bars with indoor bocce courts. Outdoor bocce courts you can drink at.

NEST
Filled with flea market antique sports trophies that he secretly imagines he won.

BEHAVIOR
Passive-aggressively jovial with turns of disproportionate competitiveness.

THREATS
Poor sportsmanship; alienating teammates/opponents/refs.

FUN FACT
They can be equally insufferable at video golf, big-game hunt simulators, Ping-Pong, and *Saved by the Bell* trivia contests.

Has no idea how to actually play this game but deadly serious about winning it

See also: Kraft Brüe Know-It-All, page 4

If elderly immigrants play it = the new hotness

THRIFT STORE QUARTERBACK

If it's more than twenty-five years old, in a hideously ugly colorway,
and associated with the losingest of losers, that jersey is a total
must-have and this species has a closet full of them.

A Super Bowl T-shirt with the wrong team declared champion is their Holy Grail

Protective eyewear against thrown elbows for cutting in the bar line

Jerseys of players embroiled in scandal and shame = score

Snap-sided weightlifter pants for quick removal when too drunk to operate a fly

MARKINGS
A mismatched pelage of memorabilia crossing eras, sports, leagues, and degrees of professionalism.

CALL
Sports banter delivered with a heavily lidded lack of enthusiasm; it's ambiguous whether they're making fun or genuinely like it.

HABITAT
Bars without televisions—they might have to publicly experience "the big game" amid emotionally engaged spectators.

DIET
Reggie! bars.

BEHAVIOR
Doesn't actually follow sports. Once every four years gets super-stoned to live-tweet Olympic curling.

PREDATOR
Actual, unambiguous, blatantly enthusiastic sports fans.

WARNING
Portraying sports fans as cartoonish morons is some deeply buried psychic revenge for being picked last for kickball.

ROLLER DERBY RAGE TORRENT

*A punny nom-de-skate cheekily referring to the violence dispensed puts
a cheeky red-lipsticked smile on the carnage.*

MARKINGS
Chipped tooth signifies "first game
opener"; neck brace indicates "end
of season."

CALL
Mouth like a sailor, that one.

HABITAT
Rented state college gymnasiums
followed by dives owned by retired
punk frontmen.

DIET
Arnica cream (for bruises);
iron nails (for spitting).

RANGE
Overlaps with Empowered
Burly-Cutie, page 72, but
prefers full-contact violence
to empowering, ironic nudity.

THREATS
Folding chairs and small children
in uncontrolled centripetal path.

SPOOR
Reek of stale sweat, dried blood,
and festering knee pads when gear
backpack is opened once a week.

MATING
Female-dominant with subservient
males acting as referees/announcers.

Body glitter makes you go faster

Keeps hated office job
for the good health
insurance. And uses
the shit out of it.

Survived
evolutionary
bottleneck of
being the subject
of an unsuccessful
Hollywood film

HARSH REALM:
The Mass Extinction

If any species can stop contemplating their navels long enough, they may start to wonder, "What came before us?" In the Genexian Era, megafauna, under the catch-all term *Slackers*, evolved to feed on a counterculture of obsessive detritus cataloging while projecting weary pessimism. Just a generation ago, their depressive, droning lo-fi call resonated across the plains and canyons of a much different environment; we can hear echoes of it in their modern descendants.

GRINDHOUSE-WORSHIPING FILM STUDENT
Died out with loss of video store habitat

In their time, the biggest threat to Slackers' existence was the pervasive but amorphous predator Corporate Culture. Primary sources discovered by scientists (*Reality Bites*, "Corporate Rock Still Sucks") show Slacker society was bonded by a primitive religion developed in fear of Corporate Culture and "not selling out." To evade its superior predation skills, different species of Slacker developed different adaptations to hide their vulnerability—a thick armor plating of postmodern distance or a defensive spray of a bleak worldview from eyes and mouth (and genitals). Ironically,* it was these adaptations that ultimately caused their demise: hopelessness and lack of trust made them slow to compete with the lithe emerging species that was able to exist symbiotically with the Corporate.

All contemporary creatures under the "hipster" umbrella are descendants of these cooperative survivors. Their adaptability to environments shaped or even poisoned by corporate effluent allowed them the leeway to create enclaves of creativity and indulgence that came to dominate the vacuum left by Slacker extinction.

*Not actual irony

GRRRL ZINESTRESS
Ancestor of the Femanish Flamewarrior

WHAT FINALLY KILLED
OFF THE SLACKER?

Two theories explain why these species died out: a massive collision of an interstellar mass nicknamed by scientists "New Sincerity" and worldwide eruption of the Internet. Streaming in from outer space, a ball of hyper-cooled self-love, pragmatism, and unqualified assumption of success burned off the nihilism-rich atmosphere Slackers needed to survive. Deprived of the defeated indifference they breathed, Slackers became weak . . . consigning them to swinging on the flippity-flop.

Before the extinction events, the magma of the Internet was already roiling in underground grottoes, with periodic spurts to the surface. With the massive eruption of Internet flows covering the surface world, the troglodyte Internet creatures' descendants would move above ground and diversify into many of the species we know today.

In the Slacker environment, dominance was determined by in-depth knowledge of obscurity. With wide rivers of free-flowing Internet carrying formerly buried obscurities above ground, the obsession-based, niche-dependent stratification collapsed as all species had equal access to resources. Old specialized habitats were flooded. Chaos reigned and the Slackers turned on themselves, destroying their era of coexistence.

AUTOBIO COMIC COLLECTOR
Defensive bony plates deflect real emotion

SLACKERS TODAY

Some Slackers have direct descendants in smaller, lighter versions that fit into new evolutionary niches. For example, the confrontational, more-anger-than-fact Grrrl Zinestress, page 80, devolved into the spineless, toothless Feman-ish Flamewarrior, page 23, to better thrive in the acidic blog biome.

However, more modern species have adopted characteristics or sport plumage and markings similar to their Slacker forebears, but at the base level their anatomy is fundamentally different. This cosmetic mimicry may either be a parallel evolution or a distraction technique rather than a vestigial holdover.

7″-ONLY BEDROOM RECORD LABEL CEO
According to legend, crowdfunding for potential documentary summary still survives

MAKE & HOARD

KOMBUCHA BREWMASTER

Modernity is far too antiseptic for this species.
Be the compost you seek in the world.

MARKINGS
No health insurance.

CALL
Theories about vaccines causing social conservatism.

HABITAT
A medical worldview alternating between nauseating panacea and tinfoil hat brigade.

DIET
All things cloudy and gelatinous.

NEST
Covered in mats. On the floor for yoga; in hair from neglect.

SPOOR
Strong musky odor of mulch and fungus piss.

BEHAVIOR
Swears by the neti pot and uses it to unblock both ends.

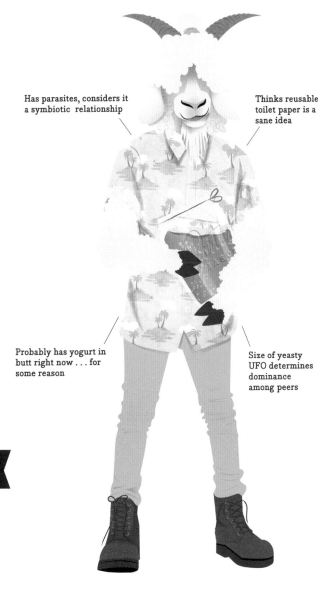

Has parasites, considers it a symbiotic relationship

Thinks reusable toilet paper is a sane idea

Probably has yogurt in butt right now . . . for some reason

Size of yeasty UFO determines dominance among peers

MATCH THE HOLISTIC SOLUTION TO THE AILMENT

GOUT	NETTLES
CONJUNCTIVITIS	POSITIVE ATTITUDE
MUNCHAUSEN	BREAST MILK
LUPUS (IT'S NEVER LUPUS)	COLLOIDAL SILVER
INABILITY TO SAY NO	CORDYCEPS
"THE BLAHS"	BLUE COHOSH
THE KING'S EVIL	COMFREY
	A BATH

TOTAL IMMERSION CRAFTER

As our world becomes less personal and more digital, this species yearns to create. Any surface not decoupaged is a wasted opportunity. All physical matter is just waiting to be reclaimed into wearable, washable, livable art.

Reclaimed/improved thrifted find

Ever prepared for spontaneous urge to knit

Still finds this hilarious

KEEP CALM AND THIS POSTER

MARKINGS
Outfit and accessories must be 85% own handiwork.

CALL
"The more stuff I hot-glue to it, the more I express my individuality."

HABITAT
Alt craft fairs that sell booze; themed meet-ups with rhymey names (stitch 'n' bitch, yarn 'n' porn); Etsy.com and/or whatever Etsy alternative isn't bankrupt at time of writing.

DIET
Twee nibbles on a hand-thrown plate decorated with '80s soap star motif (her own work, naturally).

NEST
Cluttered with carefully chosen kitsch, full of baking smells.

MATING
A primarily (but not exclusively) female species; often pairs with male-dominated species (such as Hacker/Maker/Builder/Better/Faster/Stronger Toolmaster, page 86).

ROOFTOP APIARIST

Bridging the gap between the bucolic and the urban, alongside the friendly neighborhood fire escape farmsteaders and abandoned lot terraformers, this species enables the full cycle of agriculture in one compact city block.

MARKINGS
Inadequate keeper gear—works in a wax-smeared old band shirt.

CALL
Quick to point out the bees are dying off and all life depends on them, so basically he or she is saving the world.

HABITAT
Unlicensed stall in farmers' market; niche fragrance/bespoke hardware boutique.

DIET
Honey on everything. Just don't think about what the bees are feeding on in an inner-city neighborhood of asphalt, decay, and rot, and you'll be fine.

SPOOR
$10/jar in bee season; $20/jar in winter/early spring (secretly padded with store-brand honey and antifreeze).

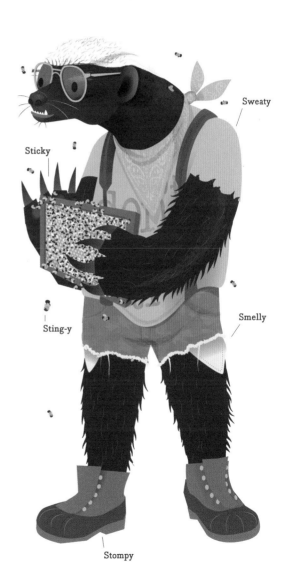

Sweaty

Sticky

Sting-y

Smelly

Stompy

HACKER/MAKER/BUILDER/BETTER/ FASTER/STRONGER TOOLMASTER

"How can I get this tall bike/giant cupcake/puppet to shoot fire?"

Resists melted polymer stains

3D-printed these from an open-source template

MARKINGS
Always in coat and gloves (fingerless, natch)—no heat in the work loft.

HABITAT
Colonies in rented loft space shared with peers; brief migration to desert festival to spawn/display.

DIET
Coffee from self-built vacuum siphon brewer (you can really taste the hydrostatic pressure!); nutritional delivery units eaten one-handed while wielding a soldering iron.

SPOOR
Leather scraps, loose Allen wrenches, melted toys.

FUN FACT
In larval phase, may briefly metamorphose into steampunk.

SEE ALSO
Total Immersion Crafter, page 84, and Architectural Salvage Upcycler, page 92, channel the same urges using yarn/junked balustrades instead of mechanical elements/flamethrowers.

VINTAGE EPHEMERA CURATOR

Everything your grandmother tossed in the trash the minute the kids moved out is now a precious collectible. Yes, that polyester twinset that your aunt barfed on in 1974. Actually, anything that was barfed on in 1974 is a must-have.

MARKINGS
Keen on the "sexy secretary" look, dismissing the patriarchal context that birthed it.

CALL
Classifies everything before 2002 as "totally retro."

HABITAT
Trendy craft markets; prescreened antique boutiques . . . likes the past without quite so much "old people smell" on it.

DIET
Certainly not what they ate in the 1950s. Ick.

NEST
Loves vintage books enough to rip them apart and hang them on the wall in IKEA frames.

SPOOR
Never-watched season three *Mad Men* box set; multiple flea market–scored sour-milk-reeking Thermoses.

The sucker willing to drop fifty bucks for some ragged Expo '86 mugs

Totally thinks she was born in the wrong decade

Repro, unforsh

OUTMODED GAME HOARDER

This species gets off on chunky pixels despite being born too late to have experienced it as the height of technology.

Tried a modern first-person shooter once; got stuck in a corner

Will never actually play but always has on display for mad props

Tattoo= ambiguous enough to be artsy rather than geeky, but peers will "get it"

MARKINGS
At least one item of dress per outfit must declare coded loyalty to some digital franchise in order to stealthily identify members of species to each other in a crowd.

CALL
Says *8-bit* when he means *16-bit*, *32-bit*, or anything other than contemporary gaming standard; chiptunes.

HABITAT
Dive bar with a functioning table-style *Ms. Pac-Man* or stand-up *Galaga*; yard sales.

DIET
Twenty-year-old *Super Mario Bros.* cereal bought in an online auction for five times the original price.

SPOOR
Modern website interfaces disguised to look like the title screen of a ColecoVision knock-off; fan art (*see also*: Pop Culture Picasso, page 99).

OBSOLETE MEDIA FETISHIST

Fetishizing data storage of a less high-powered age
as being an innate quality of its superiority.

MARKINGS
Black rings around eyes; cathode ray–warmed basement pallor.

CALL
Disappointed grumbling whenever iTunes updates again. "Why can't things stay the way they were before I was aware of them?"

HABITAT
Garage sales in the suburbs; thrift stores in unfashionable neighborhoods; your apartment making you watch something horrible.

DIET
Whatever. They don't make those chips I like anymore.

BEHAVIOR
Going misty-eyed thinking about LaserDisc; reordering text adventure 3¼" floppies; cleaning the heads.

MATING
Shows affection by making an actual hi-bias Dolby-enabled mix tape on cassette. (Good luck finding a functioning Walkman to play it on.)

SPOOR
A near-complete set of AOL trial CDs.

Vinyl has "warmth"; third-generation copied magnetic tape is . . . also good

VHSsive compulsive

Quirky dramedies that never got a decent DVD release = automatically good

FOUND AUDIO EXCAVATOR

The torrent of pop culture is so massive that this species is necessary to act as a sieve to filter out the usable from the forgettable and repurpose it to innovative/hilarious/disturbing effect.

Justifies shoplifting as an experiment in "3D creative commons"

"I think of myself as a Buchanan and Goodman for the post–Jay Z world."

Culture jamming with no culture, little jamming

MARKINGS
Milk crate–combing claws; nose for yard sales.

CALL
"All copyrights are fascism"; "Juxtaposition, remix, and appropriation is the only twenty-first-century art form."

HABITAT
Record fairs; eBay auctions; Dumpsters of nursing homes.

DIET
Incredibly varied, but most of it is crap.

SPOOR
Choice beat to loop or unexpected line of movie dialogue dropped into podcast/mix tape.

THREATS
YouTube mainstreaming the good stuff.

BEHAVIOR
Championing the virtues of "frustrating the listener"; zeroing in on the ill-advised celebrity novelty rap album.

MATING
Ruined several relationships by going into the whole U2 v. Negativland thing.

DESIGNER TOY AFICIONADO

A detached attitude of selectiveness and a preference for rarity over the mass-market distinguishes this species from mainline geek culture and the nostalgia-driven undiscriminating Brazen Kidult, page 19.

MARKINGS
Hip-hop-by-way-of-Hong-Kong exclusive brand hoodie; too many keychains.

CALL
One or more tongue-in-cheek freestyle mix tapes about a cult science fiction franchise.

HABITAT
Graphics workstation so covered with blind-box import figurines the screen is barely visible.

DIET
The packaging is all in Korean, but there's a smiling squid on it; no idea what it is.

BEHAVIOR
Alphas of the species maintain toy review and rumor blogs, collecting swag for "review" and podcasting interviews to show dominance.

SEE ALSO
Isolated populations that not only hoard factory-made toys but also frankenstein their own custom figures from dismembered limbs overlap territory with the Pop Culture Picasso, page 99.

Japan-only release, y'know

Killin' it

It's not a *toy*, it's a limited-edition collectible art piece

ARCHITECTURAL SALVAGE UPCYCLER

An Indiana Jones of downtown decay, liberating lost treasures in neglected interiors to go on to "add character" to the cookie-cutter one-bedrooms of young moderns with a love of the romantic past.

In lean times, has resorted to IKEA hacks but isn't proud of it

Trying to create a Jackson Pollock-y "smoking while making art" vibe in studio

There isn't any object made between 1920 and 1940 that can't be made into a lamp

MARKINGS
Urban spelunking gear; patina stains.

CALL
"Pssst . . . wanna buy a pergola?"

HABITAT
Zoned for demolition.

DIET
More asbestos dust and lead paint flakes than are recommended, but it's worth it.

THREATS
Landmarking committees; police responding to a B&E APB.

NEST
Welded-together shipping containers; plywood bookshelves with raw edges.

MATING
Invites potential mates to workspace to see their "etchings"; defies expectations by actually having etchings.

BEHAVIOR
Turning non-clocks into clocks.

PREDATOR
Less aesthetically inclined scavengers ripping copper wire out of walls to buy meth.

SUSTAINABLE LANDSCAPE ARCHITECT

Climate change is a foregone conclusion, and this species assists with the transition to an apocalyptic dust bowl future for the moneyed class that still wants to host garden parties.

MARKINGS
A green thumb that doesn't necessarily have to stay green year-round—that's unnatural; let a thumb have a fallow period. Brown doesn't mean dead.

CALL
"Self-seeding volunteers . . .";
"Green roof . . ."

HABITAT
Drought zones in front of $100 million vacation homes.

DIET
Low-impact "ancient grains" and lumpy seeds that they swear will be the future of farming; don't ask about the cricket flour—you don't want to know.

BEHAVIOR
Nero fiddled while Rome burned; they plant four-season low-moisture gardens while the Antarctic ice sheet crumbles.

HOST SPECIES
One percenters who finally got around to watching *An Inconvenient Truth* and who don't want to be "part of the problem" despite massive homes, cars, tech gadgets, and frequent air travel.

Missing the forest for the drought-resistant scrub trees

Went to a liberal arts college; don't refer to them as "landscapers"—they can't even speak Spanish, sheesh

THE FINER ARTS

IMMERSIVE ~~THEATER~~ THEATRE AUTEUR

*Writer-director-adaptor-actor-composer-designer-
game-changer-provacateur.*

MARKINGS

Nonperiod dress; *Eyes Wide Shut*–
style orgy mask.

CALL

"The purpose of art is not to entertain
but to challenge and upset people . . .
with a full bar."

HABITAT

Nontraditional immersive movable
performance spaces—parking lots,
condemned warehouses, fringe art
festivals . . . with full bars.

DIET

The scenery, which is minimal and
starkly evocative.

THREATS

Public indifference; live theatre's
irrelevance.

SPOOR

A Doll's House with an all-amputee
cast performed in an abandoned
mental hospital. Exploitive? No,
challenging! Can I refill this for you?

PRESS CLIPS

" . . . EMPLOYED A FASCINATING MIX OF PERFORMANCE
STYLES, FROM KABUKI TO PROLONGED SHRIEKING . . ."

"AGGRESSIVELY MEDIOCRE YET SHOCKINGLY
SELF-IMPORTANT."

"ONE WOULDN'T EXPECT A REVIVAL OF *THE MUSIC MAN*
TO HAVE QUITE SO MUCH BLOOD SPRAY IN IT . . ."

Can make any Shakespeare
play a metaphor for Nazis
somehow

Disrupts cultural
assumptions by
night; auditions for
beer commercials
by day

Spent six months stomping
and chanting with a
pioneer of 1960s off-off-
Broadway theatre (now
completely senile)

PUBLIC LITERARY SHOW-OFF

Even a friendless intellectual needs public validation.

Real paper, of course (e-readers are for airport novels)

Condescendingly looks out for mispronunciations of J. M. Coetzee or Ngũgĩ wa Thiong'o

Adores public radio; can listen to *All Things Considered* full-blast and read at the same time

MARKINGS
The same glasses frames James Joyce wore! The same kind of sweater Kerouac once owned! The same brand of loafers William S. Burroughs once OD'd in!

CALL
Thoughtful sighs and interested grunts emitted in the desperate hope that someone will ask what they're reading.

HABITAT
Cafés attached to independent book shops; bars (always alone); parks near universities (seasonal).

DIET
Green tea, preferably *yama gyokuro* . . . palate is far too sensitive for coffee.

THREATS
Freelancers with their laptops hogging all the good tables.

PUBLIC TRANSIT ART PRANKSTER

Turning the mundane into art and casting a ray of whimsical sunshine onto the workaday world is this species' mission statement; one's surreal moment of fun is another's annoying inconvenience.

MARKINGS
Carrying an inappropriate item in public; no pants.

CALL
Look at me! Look at me! Look at me! You are boring. (Words vary; meaning the same.)

HABITAT
All the world's a stage; all commuters are a captive audience.

BEHAVIOR
Doing something unusual but not technically illegal; working cake into it somehow (cake always seems to go viral).

SPOOR
Hidden camera video of entire ride posted online; coverage by bloggers who don't commute.

THREATS
Transit cops with no sense of the sublime.

FUN FACT
If it's raining out or they are feeling lazy, they can always create a fake Twitter account, anonymously tweet nonsense for two to three years, and call it a day.

Pushes the boundaries of how to annoy others, thus creating art

Ticket to the art show

In cities without transport infrastructure, she may resort to attention-seeking bicycles (tall, pinwheels, noisy)

ADVERTISING COLLAGIST GRAFFITEUR

Sees media theorist Fredric Jameson's observation "pastiche eclipses parody" as a guiding principle. Street art? More like street fart!

Repeatedly asserts that there's no art that "isn't" collage

Stencils? Psht. What are you? British and from 10 years ago?

More fiddly than tagging but you get to use razors, badass!

MARKINGS
Homemade T-shirts of nonsensical parody slogans; getaway boots for a paste-'n'-dash.

CALL
"Right now I'm super into the aesthetic power of multiples and multiplicity . . . how many dicks should I paste on her head?"

HABITAT
Subway stations and bridge overpasses closest to fashion school.

DIET
Accidently inhaled wheat paste.

BEHAVIOR
Paradigm shifting, yo. Creating mad street pieces that recontextualize media messages using their own language against them.

SPOOR
Stickers with QR code linked to inscrutable portfolio website.

PREDATORS
Harder taggers defacing their defacement.

POP CULTURE PICASSO

Not long ago, fan art was a shameful pursuit of the geekiest of the genre. Smelling an untapped potential, it was hung on the wall of galleries and in "re-contextualizing" the surroundings, a new species flourished.

MARKINGS
T-shirts displaying witty juxtaposition of pop culture themes made by peers with better marketing strategies.

CALL
"I'm totally super-famous online."

HABITAT
Pot-smoking circles behind group show openings; image-based microblogging platforms.

PREY
Suddenly moneyed young Hollywood/Silicon Valley types with more cash than taste who make purchase decisions based on "that's a picture of a thing I already know I like."

SPOOR
Decorative artifacts displaying technical skill but no reference beyond the top-10 box office hits of childhood.

GO-TO THEMES

BATMAN	POKÉMON
STAR WARS	SEXY PINUP
BACK TO THE FUTURE	BENEDICT CUMBERBATCH
GHOSTBUSTERS	TAXIDERMY
PRINCESSES	HIPSTERS
STEAMPUNK	CARTOON ANIMALS

Most preferred medium is novelty T-shirts "voted on" by the Internet

Didn't sell well; not in the moment's current cultural canon

When in doubt, steal from the best; call it a "tribute" if anyone complains

INDEPENDENT BOOK RESHELVER

This species escapes into books the way a Nazi war criminal escapes into Argentina: with an unflappable commitment to their cause and an unshakable sense of superiority.

Has to keep the Sedaris behind the counter because people keep shoplifting it

MARKINGS
A glow of contentment from just being surrounded by literature . . . the smell of a book, the feel of the pages, the crisp spines all in a row. Oh, and you can read them, too, I guess.

CALL
Overly long and meticulously lettered "Staff Recommendation" signs.

HABITAT
Non-chain specialty bookshops with a personal touch (where "personal touch" = no autobiographies by reality show stars).

DIET
Yesterday's dried-out pain au chocolat from the in-store coffee bar. Hasn't been assigned enough hours at minimum wage to pay rent *and* buy food.

SPOOR
Perfectly pyramided sales table displays.

THREATS
Being forced to admit they never actually, technically finished *Infinite Jest*.

THE HOT LITERARY PROSPECT

Whether NYC or MFA, any young writer can be a BFD.

MARKINGS
Looks quirkily handsome alongside peers in magazine photo spreads of Best New Voices of the Year.

CALL
Tortured deconstructed metaphor.

HABITAT
"30 under 30" magazine cover stories or "Next Big Thing" listicles of up-and-comers.

DIET
Champagne brunches on the publisher's dime. For now.

MIGRATION
Triangulates among retreats at Bread Loaf and Yaddo and a writer-in-residence gig at a tiny college nobody's ever heard of.

SPOOR
First novel/short film/political statistic–analyzing matrix was good enough, but no one will remember it in a year.

LIFE CYCLE
When he fails to "up-and-come," there's always teaching. Bitter, bitter teaching. Crushing the hopes of the next wave of never-wases.

Myopic in sight; macroscopic insight

Jaunty

Ivy League style; state college degree

Old (elementary) skool

BLOG-TO-BOOK EDITOR

It takes special skills to stretch a single viral infographic into 128 pages, y'know.

Crowd-sourced photos + nostalgia + pithy captions = $$$$

Hand that feeds (bitten by authors)

Missed out on getting *$#*! My Dad Says* by thaaaat f**king much

MARKINGS
A page-downing thumb callus; glazed expression.

CALL
"Lists sell. And obvious lists of common knowledge sell double"; "Make it about weed"; "Can you set it in the '80s?"

HABITAT
Positive and PR lingo–laden reviews on Amazon from burner accounts.

DIET
1,001 *Star Wars* Themed Microwave Meals; Teen Movie Cupcake Recipes.

THREATS
Snobs who prefer books with words and content; Tumblr-trolling interns jockeying for their office cube.

SPOOR
Filling discount bins everywhere the day after Christmas.

HOST SPECIES
Casual friends who feel obliged to give birthday gifts but don't know what the other is into; publishers bewildered by "youth market."

FUN FACTS
. . . is the title of the next big holiday release.

DREAM JOURNALISTA

Everyone has a great book inside them but not everyone has the sensitivity to bleed those words onto the page. Not religious but, like, really spiritual.

MARKINGS
Distinctive retinas adapted solely for the contemplation of the navel.

DIET
A reconstituted paste of Jungian archetypes and hippie-dippie self-affirmation.

HABITAT
Up their own ass.

BEHAVIOR
Belief in the creative power of "The Universe."

SPOOR
Reams of "free writing" and "morning pages."

THREATS
Actually reading any of their drivel.

MIGRATION
Saving up to go to a cabin upstate to just write for a week straight—no interruptions—but keeps blowing paycheck on incense cones and scarves.

FUN FACT
Alphas show their dominance by peacocking accessories—feather quill, manual typewriter, fountain pens.

Europe's artsiest journal mass-produced in China

Self-expression, tapping everyone's potential to channel the creative spirit using the most SAT words possible

Writes "just for myself" with no ambitions to speak to a wider world (easily met)

OUTFIT-OF-THE-DAY *EN PAPIER*

ACKNOWLEDGMENTS

For my parents, who have been subsiding my lifestyle so that I may be closer to these magnificent creatures. Infinite thanks for the insight and perspective of Sarah Wilkes and Silvija Ozols, without whom this book would be much shorter.

Published in the United States by Ten Speed Press, an imprint of the Crown Publishing Group, a division of Penguin Random House LLC, New York.
www.crownpublishing.com
www.tenspeed.com

Ten Speed Press and the Ten Speed Press colophon are registered trademarks of Penguin Random House LLC.

Some of this material has appeared in a slightly different form on hipster-animals. tumblr.com.

Library of Congress Cataloging-in-Publication Data is on file with the publisher.

Trade Paperback ISBN: 978-1-60774-791-8
eBook ISBN: 978-1-60774-792-5

Printed in China

Design by Margaux Keres

10 9 8 7 6 5 4 3 2 1

First Edition